# Marketing

*Powerful Strategies and Techniques to Make your Business Explode, Increase Sales, Make More Money and Expand Your Brand*

# Robert S. Parker

# Contents

# Chapter 1. What is the Business Mindset?

*"I truly believe in positive synergy, that your positive mindset gives you a more hopeful outlook, and belief that you can do something great means you will do something great."*

**Russell Wilson**

Many people think that the business being successful will rely solely on the business model, but this just isn't true. More importantly, if you want to have a successful business, then you will need to have a successful business mindset. The mindset that you have is extremely important because it will determine if you fail or succeed. Your own mind can hold you back from many things, but if you continue to push through you are sure to excel at anything you take on.

Being an entrepreneur is also a mindset, and it is what can launch you into the business world. Many people think that an entrepreneur is just someone that can start a business, and that is the answer most people will give you if you ask them what they think it means. Very few people will actually describe the type of person that makes up an entrepreneur.

You may hear terms sometimes that describes them as a leader, a hero, a visionary, or a risk taker. Other people think that you have to be creative, aggressive, and influential to make it big in the business world. Sadly, this is only part of it, and you don't have to be aggressive at all. You can have a quiet presence that still commands a room.

**The Inherent Will to Survive:**

Everyone is born with the ability to survive. That is what an entrepreneur is really about. It's all about survival in an evolving world, and every last person can think innovatively. All you have to do is think about your life, where you need to make a decision.

We will all come across that point in our life where we'll need to make a hard choice, and sometimes the right choice is one that has risk. There will be other times that it is better to take the road that has been traveled before. Though, most of the time you are going to need the ability to adapt to change and become fluid. This is what a successful business mindset is all about. Every time you make a decision that is for the best interest of your survival in a comfortable position, even if it is a hard road to travel at first, you are in a small way building up the mindset you need to be a true entrepreneur.

You must think and do things that you haven't done before, and each time you do so you are taking a small risk of failing. However, so long as you build up the characteristics of a mindset that will keep you persevering and chasing after your goals, it can become your safety net, allowing for your business to grow and succeed. This will also maximize your happiness, and in turn maximizing your happiness will maximize the strength of will you need to keep making these decisions no matter how big the risk becomes. The hope that is cultivated will lead you to something that is better.

**Finding What Helps You Prosper:**

You can actually build up a successful business mindset throughout your life, and it is never too late to build up a business mindset that will make starting a business that much easier. It is all about survival, but that also means building yourself up even if the world has knocked you down. Mindset will become your drive, and that is motivation in itself.

There will be a groove that you can get into from your schedule that will help you to prosper, but it is also more than a schedule. When you are building your mindset up, you will find that nothing is as simple as taking one step. It is all about the little steps that we take in the direction to our ultimate goal, which goal setting will also be important when building up your mindset and your business.

From finding the thoughts that will help you to move forward to the acts that will help you keep moving even when you feel beat down, you can find your faith in something. Having the mindset you need, also means finding faith in yourself. All of the tips and tricks to build the mindset you need and start your business with the right attitude to launch it can be found in this book, and when followed you can guarantee your own success.

# Chapter 2. Power Habits to Change Your Mindset

*"The philosophy of lifestyle design is actually quite simple. It suggests that there are limitless ways to arrange and configure your life and that the logistics of living are much more flexible than most of us can imagine."*

**Clay Collins**

Many people believe that when you fall into a rut, you are stuck in it. This is not true. Your lifestyle is a process of how you live your life, and you can change up the process at any time that you like. If you are trying to develop the business mindset to successfully launch your business, your very lifestyle will need to change in drastic ways, but it doesn't have to feel drastic. Simple power habits of a successful person will help you to become successful the more you practice.

**A Few Simple & Successful Power Habits:**

Implementing all of these habits will help to build yourself and your business up faster, but if you just implement one or two at a time, you will notice a positive change in your life that is undeniable. The speed at which you turn your life and mindset is determined by you because it is for you. You have to have the will to do something before you can turn it into a physical reality.

**Planning Ahead:**

Planning ahead is one of the easiest power habits to start, but it is one of the hardest to accomplish and follow through with. Successful people will always plan ahead because even if they take life as it comes, they need to have some sort of plan to follow. This can come naturally once you outline your goals, and outlining your goals and when you will achieve them is part of planning ahead. It is not enough to plan what you want to do in the week or month or the year.

You need to plan what you will do on a daily basis while still being able to be flexible enough to change it at a moment's notice if you are forced to without stressing out or falling into depression. If you cannot attain your goals, it is natural for it to lead into depression and even cause a lack of self-worth and that is suicide to your mindset and the successful start of your business. Being able to set day to day tasks to accomplish will help you to raise up your self-esteem and confidence, which will help to build you into the entrepreneur that you want to be and are expected to be. It can even strengthen that inherent will to survive that everyone has. These small motions will lead to bigger motions and actions, which provides a successful launch.

## Remember Time is Limited:

This is a power habit as well as a mindset tip, and you can't think that you have the rest of your life ahead of you because no one can guarantee how long that life will be. You have to grab life by the horns and direct it where you want it to go because like a bull, if you stand still it'll gore you, and you'll be left in a positon that leaves you spiraling further away from your main goals.

This is why a to-do list can be so important, and sticking to it is even more important. Outline all of your goals, especially your long term goals, breaking them into shorter goals, making sure to accomplish them on time. It's worth the sacrifice of free time if you can start to see that everything needs to be done in a timely manner to truly take the steps you need towards success.

**Go to Bed & Wake Up Early:**

It is important that you get enough sleep. Sleep doesn't just effect your physical health, but it can affect your mental and emotional health as well. The importance is often overlooked when you are trying to build up the right mindset, and not ignoring its importance will immediately set you apart from the majority. Sleep deprivation is known to actually effect your mental health as well as your physical. It can lead to stress, anxiety, and depression, which will block you from taking the steps you need to be successful.

Waking up early will also help you to make sure that you have more time in the day to complete everything that you want to, and it is more likely that you will have free time that you can devote to whatever you want. It's easier to fall into a day to day regime that will help you to succeed if you aren't feeling depressed and have the time to complete each activity. You cannot compromise with your schedule if you want to succeed, so time is of the essence.

**Let Go of Negative Thoughts:**

This is a power habit that is easier said than done, but it can be done. People should never forget that just because it's hard doesn't mean that it is impossible. You will need to learn to recognize when you are having negative thoughts, and when these negative thoughts enter your mind, you will need to dismiss them. Ask questions that will help to dismiss them. Ask yourself if you really believe what you're thinking? If you still can't see a way out of it, ask yourself if you think that it will last for the rest of your life?

The answer should always be no because nothing ever lasts forever, and you shouldn't believe in negativity if you want to be successful. This is where having faith in yourself even if you don't have faith in anything else can be an essential key to making sure that you have the tools you need to build your business and the proper mindset to be successful.

## Why It's Important:

These power habits can make a drastic change in your life if you take the time to implement them daily. These four power habits may seem simple, but ask yourself how many times you have actually followed them. The majority of people have thought about implementing these power habits, but very few of them actually get around to doing it. Start implementing these four power habits before you move onto any of the countless others that you may find. These four are easy enough to start, and it requires only small changes to how you operate. The small changes sometimes make the biggest difference with building up a mindset, especially if you have a negative one to begin with.

# Chapter 3. Tips & Tricks of the Business Mindset

*"Most of the important things in the world have been accomplished by people who have kept on trying when there seemed to be no hope at all."*

**Dale Carnegie**

Getting into a mindset for your business that will help you reach success may be the goal, but it can seem like a struggle to actually get there. No matter how hopeless or overwhelming starting a business may seem, you are able to overcome it because there is another route available for you to take if at first you don't succeed. Finding it is the hardest part, but that's why these tips and tricks will help you to further get into the mindset to further your business success.

Starting a business is a fabulous journey that will lead you to the independence that you desire with your life, but there will be both peaks and valleys along the way. It doesn't mean that those valleys have to be full of pain or even despair, but they are points where you find you need to learn more and move through as quickly as possible to reach the next peak for you and your business.

**Some Tips & Tricks to Follow:**

You need to know what to do to get into the right mindset to be successful, and it'll help make sure that you can launch your business right the first time. Even if you've already launched your business but you're struggling, then you'll find that having the right mindset will help you to sort out most of your problems. You should feel good about your business and view it properly to be successful.

**Make Sure the Products are Helpful:**

Sales are a type of service, and you need to keep that in mind if you want a successful business. Don't launch a product you know will hurt people, and that means don't sell to someone who you know can't afford something. You are truly serving people when you sell to them, and that service should be helpful.

**Mind Your Business:**

This one may seem self-explanatory, but many people don't mind their own business when they're starting their own business. There are so many things going on around you at all times, and you can't pay attention to all of them at once. Don't get into every facet of people's lives and personal dramas. It's just a distraction. When you mind your own business you can cut out these distractions, and you won't hurt yourself by inserting yourself in other people's problems. You don't have to handle any more problems than those that relate to your business, as business is a time consuming process.

**Organization Isn't an Option:**

Many people think that you can just organize later, but you can't. Remember that one power habit is to make sure that you view time as a finite thing, and that's why you have to organize as you go along. If you organize as you go along, you will be able to find everything when you need it without any hesitation. This will help you to utilize your time wisely, since you won't be wasting it trying to organize later. It can be as simple as scanning in every document to your computer as you get it, or organizing your notes once a day so that it doesn't pile up over the entire week.

Of course, you can organize more than that if you're doing digital work. Digital work is easier to organize, and there are apps and websites that can help you. You can even scan in documents as well as categorize them with different apps that are available to you on your phone. There is no excuse for being unorganized, and it'll just set you up for failure if you are.

You'll even feel more confident if you have everything where you can get to it at a moment's notice, and that's because it makes you seem like you have everything together and are on the right track, which you will. This is a part of the right mindset for the right business launch.

**Know You Can Back Track:**

One mindset that you may fall into is that you have to keep moving forward without looking back, but this isn't a helpful mindset when you are trying to launch a successful business. If you want to reach true success, you need to always be looking back to see what you could have done better. It'll help you to know what you can do better in the future, and if you have to back track to fix it, it is better to do so quickly than to try to move on until it truly becomes such a large issue that it could cause you to fail. It's better to fix things while you can, even if it's a small setback, so that you don't have to fix a bigger mess later.

## Analyze Your Mistakes:

Just like backtracking is okay, you can also admit that you were wrong. It's important that you recognize your mistakes if you want to be successful in business instead of trying to deny them. Mistakes are going to happen, and they're nothing to be ashamed of. When you recognize your mistakes, you already know that you did something wrong. Start to ask yourself how you could have avoided that mistake. Ask yourself how you could have made the situation better, and don't forget to ask yourself if you can fix it still.

If it is a mistake that you can't fix, tell yourself to let it go and move forward. You can't hold onto the mistakes that you've made if you want to be successful. Only do something if something can be done, and learn from them by analyzing what could have been done differently. You're likely going to have similar experiences in the future of your business as you do when you're just getting started, and if you learn from your mistakes you can make those experiences positive instead of negative.

**Tips Will Only Get You So Far:**

You have to remember that tips alone can't do it for you. It's up to you to act on everything that you learn from tips, tricks, and even your experiences. You have to not just learn what tips are best, but you have to implement them in your life as soon as you can. There is a mistake somewhere along the way that you've made, and you can write it down and start to see where you've gone wrong and what you could have done differently. It's a learning experience that will allow you to act on what you've learned immediately and further develop your knowledge. There is a way to implement all of these tips into your life right now, and procrastination is one way to kill success before it even starts.

# Chapter 4. A Little About Accepting Imperfect Perfection

*"Perfection itself is imperfection."*

**Vladimir Horowitz**

The first thing you need to understand when it comes to business is that nothing will be perfect. Perfection can be found in imperfection because even man is imperfect. Everything that is real is imperfect. Instead of perfection, there are many things that will go wrong with any business, epically as you're just staring. There is perfection within that imperfection, and it's something that you need to accept if you want to be able to move forward with your business and your life.

**Imperfection in Your Image:**

You are the face of your business, even if it's not your actual face that is being shown. Everything you do, including everything you say and every action you take, is important to building your brand, brand loyalty, and the general reputation that your business will run off of. You, yourself, are not a perfect person. There will be mistakes along the way, and imperfection is a type of perfection.

Remember to only strive for what you can truly accomplish. This means that you'll need to set realistic goals, which will be covered in a different chapter. When you can accept imperfection, even in your image and reputation, then you'll be able to move forward with your business. Taking the next step is always important, and you'll be too paralyzed to do so if you are trying to be a perfectionist in everything you do.

For example, if you're a writer and you get a bad review, you have to move past that bad review that you'll surely get eventually. There will always be someone that doesn't like you.

There will always be someone who dislikes your product, and that's okay. It's competition. It's life. You have to accept that imperfection to move past it.

If you were to try and dwell on that imperfection, it's likely that you'd make a mistake and keep yourself from moving in the right direction. Taking the bad review example, if you tried to reply to the bad review, you're most likely to make it worse, especially if you feel that you don't have a reason to apologize. It's best to just move on and not to reply at all.

## Imperfection in a Product:

Perfection is actually the enemy of something that is good. Of course, when you try to make a product, you want it to be as perfect as it can be. However, you should always keep in mind that something cannot be completely perfect. If you make your product go above and beyond expectations to the point that it is almost perfect, you need to realize that the money and time you put into it may make it unaffordable for the people you were originally making the product for.

Remind yourself that you can't expect perfection when you're striving to meet a goal. You can meet that goal without perfection, because there is perfection in imperfection.

Take all bad reviews or negative comments into consideration when you're looking to improve your product, but do not try to make it perfect before putting it on the market. Repeat to yourself that perfection is unattainable. Imperfection is attainable.

## Imperfection is Relatable:

Imperfection can actually be a good thing, and that's because it's relatable. Think about what you feel when you see someone who seems like the perfect person or the perfect business. It looks fake, and it often looks cooperate. If you're not actually corporate, it's okay not to have the face of the corporation. Many people will trust a company that seems to be more personal, such as a ma and pop store, rather than something that they think is a chain. This is why it's important that you stay relatable to your customers as well, and sometimes that means you'll feel a little vulnerable as well.

**It's Not Settling:**

Don't start thinking as imperfection as something that you have to settle for. Just because you move on before you make something perfect does not mean you settled with the outcome that happened. You should always make sure that you feel satisfied with imperfection and moving forward.

Choose action over perfection. You won't always be able to achieve perfection, and each day you wait is one less day that your product is out there being sold and possibly helping people. Get yourself in the mindset for imperfection, and it'll help you to continue on with your business goals.

You'll be able to jump over any hurdle that is in your way, and you'll be able to fine tune everything you want just enough to keep moving. Remember that even if you put a product out there, it isn't the end. It is never too late to go back and correct something if you need to.

# Chapter 5. The Mindset to Prioritize & Its Importance

*"I learned that we can do anything, but we can't do everything... at least not at the same time. So think of your priorities not in terms of what activities you do, but when you do them. Timing is everything."*

**Dan Millman**

One of the biggest aspects of a successful business mindset that will help you to reach success is making sure that you understand why prioritizing everything can be so important. The biggest mistake that you can start with is thinking that prioritizing means that you have to decide what will or will not get done. You should get everything you want done. So get in the mindset to prioritize, making a list is the quickest way to make sure that you knock everything out that you want knocked out.

**Making the List:**

It is important to keep a physical list of what needs to happen. This is very similar to a to-do list, and it is extremely needed. You will find that making this list and adding onto it every time you find something else you have to do will help to make sure you don't ever forget something important.

**An example of the list:**

- Get your first Kindle Book Written
- Get a Cover Made
- Get a Book Description Made
- Start a Free Promotion
- Pay my Writers

Even though paying your writers is at the bottom of the list because you thought of it last, you still need to pay your writers relatively soon. You can't pay your writers last or they won't want to work for you in the future. So then you can cross that out because it was your first priority after getting your book written, unless you are paying in advance which would mean that you reverse that.

Next, you'd need a description and then a cover before you could deal with a free promotion. Cross them out as you go, and you may have things to add to that. Such as formatting your book or anything else that it would require to be able to start that free promotion. Get it in your mind that your list's order is not the order that you should do things. You might want to number the previous list, and it helps many people to make sure that they aren't getting things out of order without having to rewrite their list all the time.

It doesn't matter where you put your list, but it should be somewhere you can take with you at all times. If you carry an agenda or small calendar with you, then you are going to want to write it there. However, many people find that it is easier to write it on your phone as many phones are now equipped with styluses as well as different notepads that you can write on and always edit. Just make sure you can change it frequently and easily, as your list isn't something finite. You will constantly be changing it, and you have to make yourself really believe that it's okay to keep your list fluctuating.

**Determining Your First Priority:**

Your first priority will always change, and that is another mindset tip that you need to get drilled into your head. Every time you knock something off your list, your first priority will change. You should have something able to readily take the place of what was once in that number one spot. This will help you to hit it hard and hit it fast.

Remember that if you use the numbering technique, all you will have to do is renumber your list. What was once your number two will become your number one priority, your number three will become your number two, and so on. Of course, this is still able to be changed as well, depending on if anything more important is added to your list. This is why you should always have a list that is easy to change, which is why once again having it digitally is recommended. It makes it a lot easier to change and modify. You have to get into a fluid mindset.

Nothing that you do is set in stone, and even when something falls through, there are other steps that you can take to get something done. When you think about your priority, it doesn't have to be your priority. If you can't pay your writers until after and they need to be paid in advance, then maybe you can pay them half in advance half on completion, or you can find a writer that works better with your schedule, for example. There is always something that you can do to shift a priority if you need to.

Your first priority should only be something that you feel needs to get done to remove an obstacle from your path to success. If it isn't removing an obstacle or helping you to take that step forward, then it shouldn't be your first priority. It can be your second priority, but things that need done that do not contribute to success should always be shifted down the list because they aren't as important as you are making them out to be.

**Don't Blow Things Up:**

Never inflate an issue and make it bigger than it actually is. This can be just as detrimental as over inflating your ego. Instead, you need to make sure that you look at each goal on your priority list for what it really is. In the example above, paying your writer means that you can keep your writer. It is not the end all if you need to get a new writer, but it can be a detriment. However, if your book promotion isn't done in the right amount of time, that isn't as big of a deal as you may want to think it is.

Remember that it's a setback that you don't have time for if you want to be timely, but it is just a setback. Every setback can be taken care of and overcome. Do not blow problems out of proportion, you'll find it's too hard to meet every goal. It can be just as detrimental as trying to reach perfection instead of finding perfection in the imperfection that you create.

# Chapter 6. Goal Setting In a Little More Detail

*"The discipline you learn and character you build from setting and achieving a goal can be more valuable than the achievement of the goal itself."*

**Bo Bennett**

A priority mindset is the first step to having a goal oriented mindset, which is also important if you want to be successful at your business. As stated in the quote above, it is important that you discipline yourself, and that means mentally as well. You can then build up your character, which will help you to achieve the goal that you want. That achievement will help you in many ways. Goal setting can be both big and small, and one of the quickest ways to failure is only setting long term or huge goals.

Those small goals are needed to help boost your confidence, and they're needed to help you reach those long term goals. If you are looking at a pile of paperwork, you need to have the tools to get that paperwork sorted. This is the same for a goal. It's just a pile of paperwork that you need to mentally sort and accomplish that sorting, and your smaller goals are your tools. You gain your tools by each goal you surpass.

## Success is Dependent On Your Goals:

Success is dependent on your goals, but it is also dependent on your goal setting ability. It's a mindset that you can accomplish, and that is by taking everything in small steps and increments at a time. For example, your main goal may be to publish ten books in two weeks. This seems like a very hard goal, and there are many ways to actually go about making sure you meet this goal. It isn't enough to actually just have that one goal. You need to then make a list of smaller goals.

Break it down. There are fourteen days in two weeks, and you need ten books. You can take four days off and get one book back a day. If you can write your own books, then this is easy enough to do. You then need to outline what you need to complete each goal. Put down details, as details will help you to turn your goals from ideas into a road map straight to success.

**Turning Each Goal Into a Roadmap:**

It's important that you create a roadmap to success, and it's easier to do then you might think. Take every goal, and outline it. You can do this mentally, but it's recommended that you actually write it down because doing that will help to make sure you don't forget even the smallest detail. If your goal is to write a book on third eye awakening, then you need to research the definition of third eye awakening. You need to come up with a table of contents. You need to figure out how to format your book, and you need to find a platform to sell it on. You also need to figure out how to promote your book and get good reviews. You need to make sure it's edited, and you may even want to outsource the writing as well as outsource a cover to put on it.

These are all the things that will need to go under your goal. You can mark each as a smaller goal that leads to your bigger goal. It will make you feel better to see each thing crossed off the list, and it'll help to direct you even when you feel overwhelmed. Never let yourself become overwhelmed if you are trying to reach success because it is the biggest mental block that you will come across.

## A Goal Warning to Follow Seriously:

It is better if you do not set too many goals at once. Many people will set a week, and a week is a good place to start. You can put your monthly and yearly goals as well, but you do not want to take and map out those goals with too many smaller ones for the entire year. There are many reasons for this, and the first is that your mindset should be telling you that these goals are not finite in how you'll achieve them, as that's the proper mindset for success in the business field. There are many ways to achieve the end that you want to. Another reason is once again you don't want to become overwhelmed.

Having all of those small goals will make it seem like you have more things to do then you really do because you would have to do each and every one of those things either way. The roadmap is to make sure that it is easier, and you'll defeat the purpose if you're not taking it one step at a time. So you'll need to look at it one step at a time. Once again, technology is usually best for this, and that's because it allows you to expand on your list without rewriting it all of the time. A simple Word document will usually be enough to create the roadmap that you need to.

**Some Final Goal Setting Tips:**

It can be still broken down into manageable sections, but there are a few more goal setting tips that will help you to reach success. You'll find these tips below, making it that much easier to be successful. Success should be hard work, but it should never be something that stresses you out enough that you block yourself from achieving everything you want to. Make it as easy as possible, and that is what these tips are meant to do.

**Always Set a Date:**

A goal without a date is relatively useless, and this is because you have no drive to make that goal come into a reality instead of just an idea in a timely manner. You should always strive to reach your goals in a timely manner, but it is also important that you make it a reasonable date. If you're writing those ten books yourself from the previous example, then it may be unreasonable to get them done in two weeks. However, it is possible if you're outsourcing. Set dates that are realistic, but also make sure they aren't too far away.

**Make Yourself Accountable:**

You need to find a way to make yourself accountable for all of your goals, and one of the best ways to do that is to make sure that you tell people. If you tell people that you are going to do it, then there is that social pressure to achieve that goal in the time you said in case someone asks. You don't want to be caught in an embarrassing situation where you tell someone that you failed, so you'll try harder naturally.

## Makes Sure the Goal Adds Meaning:

A goal should never be something that is just monotonous or something you feel you just have to do even though it won't help you out at all. A goal should have meaning towards improving your overall life, and that can be from improving your happiness or improving your financial situation which will contribute to your happiness.

Goals are extremely important, but remember that nothing is set in stone. Build a mindset that is fluid if you want to be successful, and that includes with all goals. You have to be flexible and bend with whatever the world throws out you. The more flexible your mindset is, the less likely you are to crack under pressure, allowing you to reach success a little easier.

# Chapter 7.
# Technology & Tools in Your Mind & In Your Hand

*"I'd always loved technology. It's something I always messed around with in computer labs at school. So I glommed onto it very early as way to differentiate myself in business."*

**Daniel Suarez**

Our era relies heavily on technology, and you'll need to be able to use technology to your advantage to help yourself and your business grow and become a success. You cannot have the mindset that technology isn't important or should only be used seldom. The more you integrate your business with the technology that is available to you, the more likely you are to succeed. Just repeat to yourself that learning more about the technology that is available to you is going to help you grow, and if you keep reminding yourself, it will become easier to start to learn and use this technology to help you.

**Basic Apps & the Mindset You Need With Them:**

Technology can help to make you a little more productive in your everyday life, and this translates to your business and business goals. You need to remind yourself that this type of productivity is best, and you can cut corners so long as the same results is made without sacrificing quality. That's what these basic apps will help you to accomplish.

**Evernote:**

You should always have Evernote somewhere. It doesn't matter if it's your tablet, computer, or your phone. You don't even have to pay for the basic version of Evernote, and in your business mindset you should remember that if it's free and helpful, you should have it.

It will help you by giving you a workspace that allows you to store files, documents, images, basic information, and create various forms of notes, including voice notes. It's the main place you should go for any information or thoughts you're looking for that you filed away. Your goal list can even go here because it can easily be updated and changed, and you can even share it with people.

**Sunrise:**

You need to have a calendar that will help you to achieve your goals quickly and effectively, and the basic calendar usually doesn't cut it. Remind yourself that being organized in your everyday life will help you to be more productive and successful even in the business aspect of your life. Your calendar should also be simple to follow, and that's why this app is so helpful.

**BufferApp:**

This is an app that most people don't even know about, but it's extremely useful when you're trying to make sure that you are socially active on social media networks, such as Google+, Twitter, LinkedIn, and Facebook. Promotion is key to business success, and you can always promote yourself through these social media outlets.

To create successful promotions you need to update constantly, even when you're asleep. That's what the BufferApp allows you to do. You can make your schedule work on its own by setting everything up in advance, and it'll go out when you have it timed for. To use this app, continuously remind yourself that planning in advance is best, and it'll make your life easier overall.

**Dropbox:**

Dropbox also has a free version that will work for almost anything you do, and it makes file transferring among your devices and even workers that much easier. You just drag your file to the Dropbox file app, and you'll be able to access it anywhere that you have your Dropbox downloaded and linked to. Of course, if you have internet access, you can also just access your Dropbox through their website.

You can edit files, upload images, and every screenshot you take is automatically added to your Dropbox for you to use. Not everyone you connect to your Dropbox can see everything, either. You actually have to just create a shared file between you and whoever you're working with. Remember that in your business mindset you should always be wondering how to streamline your work, especially with groups, and Dropbox allows you to do that for free.

**Apps Won't Replace Work Ethic:**

No matter what technology you are using, no matter if it's apps, software, program, new devices or anything else, it will not replace your work ethic. The biggest thing about having a successful business mindset is to make sure that your mindset never waivers on your work ethic. Technology is just meant to make it easier, but your business success will always reflect the work that you put into it. Hold yourself accountable, but allow technology to help minimize the stress and pressure of running and launching a successful business.

# Chapter 8. A Mental Check to See if You're Ready

*"I'd always loved technology. It's something I always messed around with in computer labs at school. So I glommed onto it very early as way to differentiate myself in business."*

**Daniel Suarez**

You can't move forward with your business if your head is not truly in your business. You need to be able to make sure that you have the mindset that will be able to create success instead of be a detriment to it. You need to have your head in the game so to speak, and it's more than possible. If you work at it, your mindset will become second nature, and you will no longer need to correct yourself on the habits that are becoming a detriment to you launching and managing a successful business.

## Performing a Mental Check & Questions to Ask Yourself:

You need to perform a mental check when you are about to move forward with your business, and this will help you to assess if you are ready to move onto any risk taking actions or if you're able to make any major decisions concerning the startup and launch of your business or even just furthering it. Below you will find a few questions to ask yourself before you move forward.

## Is What You're Doing Productive Towards Your Overall Success?

This is one of the most basic questions that you should always be asking yourself if you are in the proper mindset to launch and run a business. You should always be wanting to further your success, which will make you happier in your business and home life. Having the money to do what you want and make your own schedule, which having a successful business will provide, will also help to make sure that you have what you need make your life happier. Don't waste time on something that doesn't contribute to your success.

## Are You In A Positive Place With Your Thinking?

You don't have room for self-doubt or negative thoughts as a whole when you are trying to be a successful entrepreneur. You need to stay positive, and remember that one of the main factors in making anything impossible to accomplish is telling yourself that you can't do it.

## Are You Around Positive People?

This may not seem as important, but it is important in keeping a healthy mindset. You need to be able to make sure that you are around people who will cheer you on because positive energy needs to be met by positive energy to keep the outlook that will keep you motivated. Losing motivation is the best way to kill your business quickly, and if you want to keep it alive you need to keep that motivation alive. You don't need to be overwhelmed, and you certainly don't need people to believe that you can't do it because you'll start to believe them if they keep saying it.

**Do You Have The Tools Necessary To Move On?**

This is a big question that should always be posed before you take a big action. This is because without tools, you are setting yourself up for failure. No matter how confident you are, get it through your mind that you need help from devices or other people. If you don't want to rely on other people, you better have all the required tools to get the job done in your toolbox. This can be anything from the right app to the right software to even the right knowledge.

## Are You Knowledgeable About What You're Going To Do?

Your mindset should already be telling you that there is always something left to learn that will help you because that's the mindset that will help you succeed. Never think that you know it all, but ask yourself if you feel you know enough to proceed. You should be able to answer yes if you think that you can move forward.

For example, if you're publishing a book, you should know what platform it needs, basic pricing, rules and regulations, that the book's content is good, and the format it needs to be published in. that would be enough to move on. You can learn more about promotions later, how to get reviews later, or even how to respond to negative reviews later. Learning never stops, but you should always know enough to take the next step.

## Is There An Example You Can Use?

You do not need to rely on examples, and your mindset should have you feeling confident enough that you don't feel you have to. However, having an example to help refer back to is yet another tool that can go into your mental toolbox to help you succeed. Building up that mental toolbox is a mindset all on its own, and it is another facet of the general mindset for success that you're building. Use examples when you have them, and if you need a little more help, always remember to seek examples out.

**Preparing Your Mental Toolbox From Your Mental Check:**

The right mindset is what makes a mental check possible. You need to feel positive, and you need to be able to check everything off your list. However, you also need to check your mental toolbox. Make sure that you have every tool necessary to help you. Some examples are the technology, as we discussed above, but you also need to have the rudimentary skills or knowledge to move forward and perhaps a network of people that you can talk to. This can be anyone from someone who has prospered in the business to a forum of people who are trying to reach the same goal that you are.

# Chapter 9. Work Ethic as a Key Point & Habit

*"At the end of the day, you are solely responsible for your success and your failure. And the sooner you realize that, you accept that, and integrate that into your work ethic, you will start being successful. As long as you blame others for the reason you aren't where you want to be, you will always be a failure."*

**Erin Cummings**

You are the only one who can create success in your life. Success will not be handed to you, but it is still extremely possible to achieve. It's within your reach, but you have to reach and stretch for it. This means stretching your physical capabilities as well as your mental ones, where you build your knowledge and mental toolbox to achieve the success in your business that you desire.

You have to integrate work ethic into everything you do because the amount of work you put into launching and maintaining a business will then be translated into the success of that business. You cannot blame others for your failure, and you certainly can't give them credit for all of the hard work that you put into your everyday life. Make sure that you're where you want to be because it is only you who are responsible for your failure if you aren't.

## Characteristics of a Good Work Ethic:

The mindset described above about taking responsibility for your actions and your success is what will help you to develop the work ethic you need. However, you still need a measurement of what a good work ethic will be. The benefits of a good work ethic will be explained later, but it will benefit you directly. If you are used a work ethic that is productive, then it'll even help to minimize the stress that you feel.

**Cooperation:**

You have to be in a work environment that cooperates with your goals, and this means that you are ready to go where you need to so that you may create this work environment. Make sure that you have a beneficial environment, and that if you are working with anyone else you have an environment that will meet both of your needs. This is a sign of having a good work ethic that will help you to solve any problems that you may come across.

**Productivity:**

The first thing you'll notice to help you judge if you have a good work ethic or not is to be able to judge your productivity. Ask yourself if you are meeting all of your goals in a timely manner, and if so then your productivity doesn't need to be worked on. If not, you need to find what will help you to increase your productivity. Often, positive thinking to help contribute to the right mindset is the best place to start.

**Character:**

If you have a good work ethic, you'll find that your character is being built up. Other people may notice it before you, and this is partially due to the new and improved mindset that you are building as well. You can self-reflect on your discipline to help build up your mindset more as well, and this will in turn build up your character. Remember that staying honest and trustworthy isn't an option if you want to become and remain a successful business owner. It is necessary for you to build up a client base and customer loyalty, no matter what business you're in. you need to demonstrate honesty and reliability daily, and it can't be just when you have a client around.

## Dedication:

You always need to ask yourself if your mindset is making you dedicated to your work or not. If it is not making you feel dedicated and motivated, then you do not have a successful mindset, and it means you will not have a successful work ethic. Dedication is going to be your driving force, and you need to remind yourself that your dedication is something that will actually pay off. Your dedication directly translates into your work ethic and how much you get done, meaning it determines how far you move forward with your business. This is key to success, so always keep in mind that dedication is needed as a step towards launching and maintaining a successful business.

## The Benefits of a Good Work Ethic:

Sometimes staying in the right mindset is extremely hard on you, and it can be taxing before it becomes a habit. It'll be easier after it becomes a habit, but sometimes it's best to

remind yourself why building up a piece of that
needed mindset is going to be beneficial. You'll
find the reasons that a work ethic is beneficial
to your mindset and overall business goals
below.

- If you have a good work ethic you are
  more likely to remain in a productive
  pattern throughout your work days, even
  if you're not on a particular schedule.

- If you already have a good work ethic,
  you are less likely to become stressed or
  anxious over your work, which will stave
  off depression. By minimizing the
  likelihood of that stress, you are also
  able to continue with productivity,

keeping the mindset you need, and keeping yourself moving forward in your business plans.

- If your work ethic is already good, then you are more likely to start your days early and get everything done on time. This will leave you more time to spend with your family, friends, or just doing what you love. In turn this will help to increase positivity in your life, which will then increase the positivity in your mindset which also leads to success.

- If you have a good work ethic, then you're less likely to fall behind in your work, allowing you to meet all work related goals. The ability to meet goals boosts your confidence, which in turn will help to strengthen your successful mindset and minimize stress. It will also help you to continuously grow your business instead of falling stagnant or getting very little progress accomplished in a long period of time. Making leaps and bounds in the progress of your business will help you to maintain your business, as growth is always necessary.

Always remind yourself of the benefits of keeping a better mindset and all that comes with it, and this in turn will make it easier to keep that mindset because of the positivity. It is a cycle that once you get started will start to feed into itself, which is what makes it easier in the long run.

# Chapter 10. A Few Mental Tricks to Remember

There are still many tips and tricks that you can keep in mind to build up your mindset and further the launch of your business while helping you to reach your general goals of success. You'll find these tips and tricks below, but remember that getting that mindset started is the hardest part, and so you shouldn't give up because it will become easier.

**Set Your Routine:**

No matter what you do, you need to set your routine and stick with it. This is the only way to change your mindset. Your mindset will not be changed if you are falling in and out of a routine. Repetitiveness is what helps to drill new ideas and habits into your head, and it will then become second nature. You have to work for something to become second nature.

For example, if you're learning to play the piano, you won't be able to do so without a routine. It won't become second nature to play the piano until after that routine and repetitiveness has been established, and then what you learn will become second nature. However, there will still be much more to learn, and you'll need to keep progressing just like in a business.

## Remind Yourself of the Reward:

This can be a little harder, but like it was discussed in the previous chapter, each positive habit that helps you to get into a successful mindset has a reward. That reward is usually the successful mindset, but it can also be stress reduction or allowing you to spend more time with your family. It can become easier to change your habits if you know you will get a reward for doing so. If you are having a hard time or feel stuck, then just remind yourself of that reward. This can help you to stay motivated throughout the entire process.

## Set Reminders:

You also will need reminders of what to do, and this can be as little as having that to-do list in front of you. You can even post it somewhere that you'll always see. You don't need someone to remind you what you have to do, but you are capable of reminding yourself. It's easy to forget to do something, especially if the task seems daunting as it is.

You need to remind yourself that is worth doing and that you have committed to doing it. Even reminders on your phone will work. You can set an alarm for the middle of the day, and instead of putting and appointment in the reminder slot put one of your main goals for the day. This will make sure that you do not neglect your goals or what you have to do to reach them.

## Remember to Introduce Positivity:

It isn't enough to just avoid negativity in your life when you're trying to make a large positive change, such as with changing your mindset. You also need to introduce positivity with your life. This doesn't mean that you have to start putting up motivational posters that you don't really agree with. However, it does mean that you need to try to calm yourself when you start to get anxious and repeat positive things to yourself when you feel overwhelmed.

Throughout this entire book you have learned about possible positive habits that you can develop and keep, and all positive habits will contribute to the mindset you need to be successful. Many people will introduce meditation into their daily routine, but this isn't necessary even if it can still be helpful. Just find a way to calm yourself down, stay motivated, deflect negativity in your life, and increase the positivity in your life, even if it's just from yourself.

**Don't Ignore Failures:**

Failures are a learning experience, and you are bound to fail eventually. Just remember that if you fail on one goal, there is another way to go about trying to reach that goal again and being successful with it. To find that alternative path, you are going to need to reflect on your failures. With a positive mindset you recognize that failures are bound to happen, but you also recognize that you do not have to be content with them. You just have to accept them and keep moving forward. However, even though you keep moving forward, it doesn't mean that you ignore what caused the failure to begin with.

If you have failed in a way you don't understand, then write out what you were trying to accomplish and what you did to try and accomplish it. You obviously failed, but look at what you did and see if you can determine what caused it in your actions. If you can't find any reason for your failure in your direct actions, then you probably set yourself up for failure by not having the proper mindset when taking those actions.

**Keep Moving Forward:**

Never accept failure as the end to your plans. Always keep moving. If you have the correct mindset for success, which this book has helped you to build or at least know how to build, then you will be able to keep moving with ease. However, even when it gets tough you are now equipped with what you need to handle that stress, anxiety, and break down what you need to do in smaller increments so that you can accomplish everything you want one step at a time. Remember to be realistic, and this is will help you to move forward at a steadier pace.

Remain positive, motivated, dedicated, and keep your character where you'd want any of your future employees characters to be so that you don't stop moving. If you are someone that can be relied on, then you can rely on yourself to get what you need done. You can be both the boss and the employee, and success is always within reach with the proper outlook and mindset to help.

www.ingramcontent.com/pod-product-compliance
Lightning Source LLC
Chambersburg PA
CBHW061005050726
47592CB00003B/1357